just

A LITTLE BOOK OF LIQUID PARADISE

TROPICAL DRINKS.

Cheryl Charming

Photographs by Susan Bourgoin

Lyons Press
Guilford, Connecticut

An imprint of Globe Pequot Press

Copyright © 2010 by Morris Book Publishing, LLC

The following manufacturers/names appearing in *Just Tropical Drinks* are trademarks:
Alizé® Red Passion, Angostura®, Appleton's®, Bacardi®, Baker's German Sweet Chocolate, Bénédictine, Captain Morgan® Spiced Rum, Clément, Coco Lopez®, Cointreau®, Curaçao, Demerara, DiSaronno® Amaretto, Galliano, Karo, Meyer, Midori, Peter Heering Cherry Heering, Perrier Jouet, POM Wonderful LLC, St. James, Trader Vic's

Photos on the following pages are courtesy of Shutterstock.com: page 12 © Vibrant Image Studio, page 76 © Mr. Brown.

Prop Credits:
Bar tools and products provided by www.barproducts.com.
Cocktail sticks, picks, straws, and drink decoration novelties provided by Spirit Foodservice, Inc. (www.spirit foodservice.com).

Text design by Georgiana Goodwin

Library of Congress Cataloging-in-Publication Data
Charming, Cheryl.
  Just tropical drinks : a little book of liquid paradise / Cheryl Charming ; photographs by Susan Bourgoin.
    p. cm.
  ISBN 978-1-59921-899-1
  1. Cocktails. 2. Bartending. I. Title.
  TX951.C4677 2009
  641.8'74—dc22

                                                                                2009043599

Printed in China

10 9 8 7 6 5 4 3 2 1

CONTENTS

Blenders can range in price from $20 to $2,000.

One that will last on your home counter for fifty years
should have at least 2 horsepower and cost around
$300. It's worth the investment to purchase a good
blender. The $30–$60 blenders found at local stores
burn out their motors too fast and will leave you
frustrated.

BLENDING

Cracked or small ice works best when making drinks
in a blender. When blending, add your liquid ingredients first, then slowly add ice. Start with less ice
than you think you need because you can always add
more. Strive for a pourable consistency, but if you go
a notch over the thickness, simply use a bar spoon to
help the mixture into the glass. You can use a blender
to puree as well ●

If you are a green eco-enthusiast, search for
bike blenders that hook up to a stationary
bike. There are also gas-powered tailgate
blenders for the outdoor enthusiast.

You've gone through all the trouble of concocting the perfect frozen or tropical drink for your guests.

Why ruin the effect with the wrong glass? Here is a short list of the glassware that is easy to find and will make the biggest impression.

HURRICANE GLASSES

When you see a hurricane glass, you should think of Pat O'Brien's and New Orleans in the 1930s because that's where it originated. Today in New Orleans hurricane glasses are everywhere and are available in every color imaginable, but the most prized is the souvenir glass at Pat O'Brien's. It's a 26-ounce glass with the Pat O'Brien's logo. It will hold $10 in pennies. Hurricane glasses can measure 12-26 ounces. They are often used as a festive souvenir glass and are plentiful in plastic and glass. The shape of the glass was inspired by hurricane lamps. These glasses are often used for frozen and tropical drinks.

POCO GRANDE GLASSES

Poco grande glasses can measure 10–13 ounces.
Stems on the poco grande can vary in shape, but the
curvy shape of the bowl will stay the same. Some
people call this glass a "tulip glass." These glasses are
another good choice for frozen and tropical drinks.

TIKI MUGS

Modern tiki mugs exploded and flourished in the
golden age of tiki, which was between 1933 and
1973. There were tiki bars, lounges, and rooms with

a wide assortment of exotic tropical drinks on their menus. A tiki drink was usually accompanied by extravagant garnishes and decorations, such as paper umbrellas, Chinese back scratchers, tropical flowers, sugarcane sticks, dry ice to create mist, and fruit and more fruit. Tiki mugs are in a world all their own. You find tiki skulls, Easter Island heads, fruit-shaped mugs, volcano mugs, barrels, figures, and more! Tiki mugs can measure 7–20 ounces.

Over thirty varieties of tiki mugs are available in many shapes and sizes.

The word *tiki* refers to a carved statue of a Polynesian god. Tiki mugs are usually ceramic and made by slip casting in a plaster mold, then dried, glazed, and fired in a kiln.

MARGARITA GLASSES

Margarita glasses can measure 8–16 ounces. Because margaritas can be served straight up, on the rocks, or frozen, there is a variety of glassware to choose from. The margarita glass with the salt, ice, and lime in the photo is supposed to resemble a sombrero. You can also look for some Mexican glass margarita glasses to be truly authentic ●

The most popular garnishes for tropical drinks often involve the pineapple.

Whatever the reason, know that you will need a larger space than normal when cutting a pineapple. And a larger knife. You can also save the top end of the pineapple (with the fronds). It can be used as decoration in a display or bamboo-skewered fruit kebabs could stick into it. The fronds can also be torn off and used as a garnish. You'll have to trim the bottoms of them a little for the sake of visual presentation. You can also spear fronds on a pineapple slice. A fancy way to attach the fronds to a pineapple slice is to make an incision in the top of the slice, then insert a couple of fronds down into the incision point side up. For punches made with pineapple juice, just throw a handful of fronds in for fun.

Drinks that could get a pineapple slice garnish are Piña Colada, Singapore Sling, or any tropical drink made with pineapple juice.

CUTTING A PINEAPPLE

Step 1: Begin with a secure, clean surface. Slice off the ends of a pineapple. Carefully cut the pineapple in half lengthwise. Discard the ends.

Step 2: Lay the pineapple halves flat for cutting stability. Slice both pineapple halves lengthwise. The result will be four lengthwise pineapple quarters. After some practice, you may discover that you prefer to cut the quarters in half to make eighths. This will yield more slices in the end.

Step 3: Firmly hold down a pineapple quarter (because the outside curve of the pineapple is unstable). Make a careful ¹/₂-inch lengthwise slice into a pineapple quarter. This slice allows the slice to rest on the rim of a glass. Repeat with the other three pineapple quarters. The result will be four lengthwise pineapple quarters with rim slices.

Step 4: Turn the pineapple quarter on its flat, stable side, then hold firmly. Make many slices widthwise. Repeat with the other three pineapple quarters. The

result should be 30–40 pineapple slices that will rest on the rim of a glass.

ADDITIONAL GARNISHES

The top four garnishes are lemons, limes, olives, and maraschino cherries. From that foundation a tower of garnishes can be built. Next in line would be oranges, pineapples, strawberries, and mint. There's really no limit when it comes to garnishes. You might try peaches, grapes, mango, wild hibiscus flowers, orchids, rose petals, berries, pears, apples, kiwi, watermelon, cantaloupe, bananas, basil, rosemary, sugared ginger, and sugarcane sticks.

Nonedible additions to a drink are called "decorations" and "tools." Sometimes the decorations can serve as a tool, such as a paper parasol speared with a cherry. There are unlimited choices when it comes to straws, picks, and stir sticks.

Some drinks automatically get a certain garnish. Limes are used for Margaritas and Cuba Libres. Lemons are used for teas (Long Island, Long Beach, and so forth), and orange flags are used for sours (Tom Collins, Whiskey Sour, and so forth).

MAKING FLAGS

Originally a flag was an orange slice that was speared with a cherry. Today a flag is anything that has been speared with a cherry. You can cut and spear the fruit anyway your heart desires. Look for fun and interesting cocktail picks to make flags ●

Nothing says "paradise" quite like a tropical drink in a fancy glass with a little umbrella.

These libations are dreamt about by anyone who longs to get away from the daily grind. While you may not be able to hop on the next flight to the islands, you can certainly create a little liquid vacation by cutting up some pineapple and pouring in the rum. You'll find lots of cocktail classics and modern variations in these pages.

Did you know that the Mojito was popular in the early 1930s? During Prohibition, famous writers (think Hemingway), artists, musicians, and soon-to-be famous starlets made their way down to Havana to party. And they all drank Mojitos. The Cuba Libre ("Free Cuba!") was created during the Battle of Santiago in 1898. Legend has it that Teddy Roosevelt and his Rough Riders were drinking Cuba Libres and brought the drink back to New York ●

Classic Daiquiri

INGREDIENTS

Ice
1½ ounces light Cuban rum
1 ounce fresh squeezed lime juice
½ ounce simple syrup

1. Chill a 4–6-ounce cocktail glass with ice.

2. Shake ingredients with ice.

3. Strain into the chilled cocktail glass.

Like the margarita, the daiquiri has a simple foundation based on minimal ingredients: rum, fresh lime juice, and simple syrup. The daiquiri is of Cuban descent (there's a town named "Daiquiri"), and as you might have guessed, many people claim to have invented the drink. As far as we know the term was first seen in print in 1898.

Today most people think that the definition of daiquiri is "frozen drink." This is untrue. Yes, a daiquiri can be made frozen (see page 87), but it must have all three of the base ingredients. So, for example, you can never define a Piña Colada as a daiquiri because it does not contain lime juice.

Mojito

INGREDIENTS

Fingertip full of mint leaves
$1/2$ a lime, cut
Ice
$1^1/_2$ ounces Cuban light rum
1 ounce simple syrup
4 ounces soda water
Sprig of mint garnish

1. Muddle the mint and limes in a double old-fashioned glass.

2. Fill with crushed or cracked ice.

3. Pour in the rum, simple syrup, and soda water.

4. Stir and add garnish.

> When making vintage rum cocktails like the Mojito, feel free to experiment with different kinds of rums. A gold or aged rum will give the Mojito more depth.

Skinny Mojito

INGREDIENTS

Handful of mint leaves
1 ounce lime juice
Ice
1$^{1}/_{2}$ ounces light rum
1 ounce sugar-free simple syrup
Soda water
Mint sprig garnish

1. Muddle the mint and lime juice in a tall glass.

2. Fill with cracked or crushed ice.

3. Pour in the next two ingredients, then stir.

4. Top with soda water and stir. Add garnish.

Are you tired of drinking your favorite alcohol with diet cola or plain soda water to avoid the sugar? It doesn't have to be that way. You can make practically every cocktail (and your favorites) without sugar. One trick is to replace the sugar with sugar-free simple syrup.

Blueberry Eco-Mojito

INGREDIENTS

Handful of organic mint leaves
Handful of organic blueberries
1 ounce lime juice
Ice
1^1/$_2$ ounces organic rum
1 ounce organic raw simple syrup
Filtered charged water or organic soda water
Organic blueberry and mint garnish

1. Muddle mint, blueberries, and lime juice in a tall glass.

2. Fill with cracked or crushed ice.

3. Pour in the next two ingredients, then stir.

4. Top with filtered charged water. Add garnish.

For the Blueberry Eco-Mojito, you could make infused mint rum (see page 117). If you don't care for blueberries, then simply replace them with another favorite fruit such as organic strawberries, blackberries, peaches, or black cherries.

Wild Hibiscus Mojito

INGREDIENTS

3 wild hibiscus flowers in syrup and 3
  peppermint sprigs
1 ounce peppermint leaf and Persian lime zest-
  infused light rum
1 ounce fresh Persian lime juice
1 ounce wild hibiscus syrup
Ice
4 ounces fresh charged filtered water
1 ounce gold rum
Peppermint stem, inside-out wild hibiscus
  flower garnish

1. Muddle flowers and peppermint in a tall
   glass.

2. Add infused rum, lime juice, and syrup. Fill
   with ice and fresh charged filtered water.

3. Float gold rum. Add garnish.

Cuba Libre

INGREDIENTS

Ice
2 lime wedges for garnish
6 ounces cola
2 ounces light rum

1. Fill a tall or highball glass with ice.

2. Squeeze one juicy lime wedge over the ice and discard.

3. Add the cola and rum.

4. Squeeze the second lime and drop in the drink. Stir.

Flavored rums such as vanilla, coconut, spiced, or banana can add a nice modern twist to a Cuba Libre.

Skinny Pirate

INGREDIENTS

Ice
1¹/₂ ounces Captain Morgan spiced rum
5 ounces diet cola

1. Fill a highball glass with ice.

2. Pour in the ingredients.

A lot of flavored soda waters have hit the market recently and can be a little deceiving. Beware if the front label promises "Fat Free" because all sugar is fat free; but your body converts the sugar into fat. Always make sure you turn the bottle over and read the label if there's sugar in it.

Milk Punch

INGREDIENTS

Ice
2 ounces light rum
1 ounce simple syrup
4 ounces whole milk
Nutmeg and cinnamon for garnish

1. Fill a 12-ounce glass with ice.

2. Add ingredients and stir.

3. Garnish with nutmeg and cinnamon.

4. For more flavor, you can substitute the light rum for dark rum.

Guys and Dolls

In the 1955 film, *Guys and Dolls,* Marlon Brando takes church lady Jean Simmons to Cuba on a date. At dinner, he orders Milk Punches. Jean asks about the flavoring in the Milk Punch, and he tells her that at night they put a preservative called "Bacardi" in the milk. She drinks several of them.

Hurricane

INGREDIENTS

Ice
2 ounces light rum
2 ounces dark rum
2 ounces red passion fruit syrup
1 ounce orange juice
1 ounce pineapple juice
1 ounce fresh lime juice
Pineapple or orange flag garnish

1. Fill a hurricane glass with ice.

2. Shake ingredients with ice.

3. Strain into the glass. Add garnish.

Whiskey was in short supply when Prohibition ended in 1933. This was due to the whiskey distilleries having been closed for thirteen years; also, whiskey takes time to age. Rum was abundant, so if a bar owner wanted a case of whiskey he had to buy up to fifty cases of rum. That's how the Hurricane was born; huge hurricane glasses were filled with lots of rum and juices for tourists and sailors.

Zombie

INGREDIENTS

1 ounce gold rum
1 ounce 151 Demerara rum
1 ounce light rum
1 ounce lemon juice
1 ounce lime juice
1 ounce pineapple juice
1 ounce passion fruit syrup
1 teaspoon brown sugar
1 dash Angostura bitters
Ice
Mint sprig garnish

1. Pour everything into a shaker tin without ice and stir until the sugar dissolves. Add ice, then shake and strain into the glass—a tiki or tall glass.

2. Add garnish.

The Zombie was served at the 1939 New York World's Fair.

Tiki Traffic Cone

INGREDIENTS

Orange juice straw cone
Ice
1½ ounces dark rum
½ ounce orgeat syrup (or Amaretto)
1 ounce red passion fruit syrup
1 ounce pineapple juice
1 ounce lime juice

1. Place the straw cone in a highball glass wide enough to fit the cone.

2. Shake all the ingredients with ice.

3. Strain into the glass.

> Make your own ice cone by packing a paper snow cone cup with crushed ice, adding the juice, and sticking a chopstick in the middle to make a hole for the straw.

Trader Vic Mai Tai

INGREDIENTS

Ice
1 ounce aged Jamaican rum (like Appleton's)
1 ounce amber Martinique rum (like St. James or Clément)
½ ounce orange Curaçao
½ ounce orgeat syrup (French almond syrup)
½ ounce fresh lime juice
1 ounce Trader Vic's rock candy syrup (or commercial simple syrup)
Mint sprig garnish

1. Fill a double old-fashioned glass with ice.

2. Shake ingredients with ice.

3. Strain into the glass. Add garnish.

Trader Vic owned a small grocery in San Francisco and worked as a waiter. He opened a tiki bar across the street from his grocery store and invented the Mai Tai. He was the first to open a chain of tiki bars.

Copycat Mai Tai

Ice
1/2 ounce triple sec
1/2 ounce Amaretto
2 ounces sweet-and-sour mix
2 ounces pineapple juice
1 ounce light rum
1 ounce dark rum
Pineapple and cherry garnish

1. Fill a tropical glass with ice.

2. Shake ingredients (except the dark rum) with ice.

3. Strain into the glass.

4. Float dark rum on top. Add garnish.

The term *mai tai* is Tahitian for "out of this world." The original recipe is slightly different from the recipe created for the Trader Vic's chain due to availability of products. When bartenders not working at Trader Vic's are asked to duplicate the recipe, they are limited to the standard products behind their bars, a limitation that begat the Copycat Mai Tai.

ON THE ROCKS

Blue Hawaii

Ice
$^3/_4$ ounce Puerto Rican rum
$^3/_4$ ounce vodka
$^1/_2$ ounce Bols blue Curaçao
3 ounces pineapple juice
1 ounce sweet-and-sour mix
Orchid garnish

1. Fill a tropical glass with ice.

2. Shake ingredients with ice.

3. Strain into the glass.

4. Add garnish.

Harry Yee, a veteran bartender working at the Hawaiian Village in the 1950s, was asked by Bols to help promote its blue Curaçao, and the Blue Hawaii was born. When asked about the orchid garnish, his answer was, "We used to use a sugarcane stick, and people would chew on the stick, then put it in the ashtray. When the ashes and cane stuck together it made a real mess, so I put the orchids in the drink to make the ashtrays easier to clean."

Blue Hawaiian

INGREDIENTS

Ice
1 ounce light rum
$\frac{1}{2}$ ounce blue Curaçao
3 ounces pineapple juice
1 ounce sweet-and-sour mix
Pineapple flag garnish

1. Fill a tropical glass with ice.

2. Shake ingredients with ice.

3. Strain into the glass.

4. Add garnish.

Singapore Sling

Ice
1½ ounces gin
½ ounce Peter Herring Cherry Heering
¼ ounce Cointreau
¼ ounce Benedictine
2 ounces pineapple juice
1 dash Angostura bitters
¼ ounce grenadine
½ ounce lime juice
2 ounces soda water
Pineapple or orange flag garnish

1. Fill a tropical glass with ice.

2. Shake ingredients (except soda water) with ice.

3. Strain into the glass. Add soda water.

4. Add garnish.

> The Singapore Sling was created at the Raffles Hotel in Singapore at the turn of the twentieth century by Chinese bartender Ngiam Tong Boon to attract women, so it was 100 years ahead of the cosmopolitan.

Sloe Boat to China

INGREDIENTS

Ice
1 ounce sloe gin
1 ounce white crème de cacao
4 ounces soda water
Chocolate-dipped fortune cookie

1. Fill a tall glass with ice.

2. Shake the next two ingredients with ice.

3. Strain into the glass, then top with soda water. Add garnish.

Everyone loves fortune cookies because they add a sense of whimsical magic. Why not dip some in chocolate? You could even add sprinkles and other decorations to them. Sloe Boat to China is the perfect tall, cool drink to set a dipped fortune cookie on its rim.

Bahama Mama

Ice
1 ounce coconut rum
1 ounce light rum
2 ounces orange juice
2 ounces pineapple juice
$1/2$ ounce grenadine
Pineapple or orange flag garnish

1. **Rocks:** Shake ingredients with ice. Strain into a tropical glass filled with ice. Add garnish.

2. **Frozen:** Blend ingredients with a half cup of ice. Pour into a tropical glass. Add garnish.

No one knows who invented the Bahama Mama, but it came from the Bahamas in the 1980s. It can be made many ways with many ingredients as long as you keep the same flavor profile, which is a cross between a Piña Colada and a Rum Punch.

Black Leather String Bikini

INGREDIENTS

Black shoestring licorice
Ice
2 ounces coconut rum
5 ounces white cranberry juice

1. Slowly spiral black shoestring licorice into a tall glass as you add ice.

2. Shake ingredients with ice.

3. Strain into the glass.

The Black Leather String Bikini is a simple drink that smells like suntan lotion. If you prefer a Red Leather String Bikini, simply use red shoestring licorice in place of the black.

Yellowbird

INGREDIENTS

Ice
1 ounce light rum
1 ounce Galliano
$\frac{1}{2}$ ounce banana liqueur
2 ounces pineapple juice
2 ounces orange juice

1. Fill a tall glass with ice.

2. Shake ingredients with ice.

3. Strain into the glass.

Tuscany Nectar

Galliano is a yellow Italian liqueur housed in a tall bottle—so tall that you'd think that the liqueur was invented in Pisa. And you'd be close. It was created in the Tuscan province of Livorno next to Pisa. Galliano is made with thirty herbal ingredients, including star anise, vanilla, citrus, and ginger. It was created in 1896 and named after Italian war hero Giuseppe Galliano.

Skinny Long Island Iced Tea

INGREDIENTS

Ice
1/2 ounce vodka
1/2 ounce gin
1/2 ounce rum
1/2 ounce tequila
Cap of orange extract
1 ounce lemon juice
1 ounce sugar-free simple syrup
Splash of diet cola
Lemon garnish

1. Fill a tall glass with ice.

2. Shake all the ingredients (except the cola) with ice.

3. Strain into the glass.

4. Top with diet cola. Add garnish.

Extracts can be found in the spice aisle at your local grocer. Because they don't contain sugar, you can use them to add flavor. The orange extract takes the place of the triple sec that would normally be in the Long Island Iced Tea.

Watermelon Kiwi Cooler

INGREDIENTS

Ice
4 ounces dry white wine
1 ounce lemon juice
4 ounces lemon-lime soda of choice
Watermelon balls and kiwi slices garnish

1. Fill a wine glass half with ice.

2. Add all the ingredients and stir. Add garnish.

3. You can substitute the lemon-lime soda for sugar-free lemon-lime soda.

Provide toothpicks to make it easier to eat the garnish.

Strawberry Pom Lemonade

INGREDIENTS

Ice
1½ ounces strawberry vodka
1 ounce pomegranate juice
½ ounce handmade lemonade
Lemon and strawberry garnish

1. Fill a tall glass with ice.

2. Shake all the ingredients with ice.

3. Strain into the glass. Add garnish.

Passionate Summer Holiday Sangria

INGREDIENTS

1 750-milliliter bottle red wine
½ cup Alizé Red Passion liqueur
½ cup pineapple juice
½ cup lemon juice
¼ cup honey syrup
1 pint strawberries and 1 cup seedless grapes
Ice
24 ounces pink Champagne

YIELDS 8 SERVINGS

1. Pour first five ingredients into a pitcher. Stir.

2. Add some of the fruit.

3. When ready pour 6 ounces sangria into fruit-garnished wine glasses half filled with ice.

4. Top each glass with 3 ounces pink Champagne.

Midnight at the Oasis Sangria

INGREDIENTS

1 750-milliliter bottle red wine
$\frac{1}{2}$ cup pineapple vodka
$\frac{1}{2}$ cup tangerine juice
$\frac{1}{2}$ cup lemon juice
$\frac{1}{4}$ cup raw sugar or raw sugar simple syrup
2 oranges, 1 cup pineapple fronds, pineapple, and 1 star fruit
Ice
24 ounces lemon-lime soda

YIELDS 8 SERVINGS

1. Pour first five ingredients into a pitcher. Stir.

2. Add oranges and pineapple.

3. When ready pour 6 ounces sangria into fruit-garnished wine glasses half filled with ice.

4. Top each glass with 3 ounces lemon-lime soda.

Tropical Hibiscus

INGREDIENTS

Ice
1 ounce mango rum
1 ounce cranberry juice
1 ounce pineapple juice
$\frac{1}{2}$ ounce hibiscus syrup
3 ounces dry sparkling wine or brut Champagne
Sugarcane stick and a wild hibiscus flower
  turned inside out for garnish

1. Fill a tall glass with ice.

2. Shake the first four ingredients with ice.

3. Strain into the glass, then top with sparkling wine. Add garnish.

Wild about Hibiscus Flowers

Lee Etherington was the first to use the Australian wild hibiscus flowers in cocktails. It began at a dinner party in 1998 when he dropped a flower into a glass of Champagne. Before then the flower had been used as a popular Australian dessert garnish. Soon after, Lee started the Wild Hibiscus Flower Company, which preserves his flowers in natural syrup for worldwide availability.

Stop and Smell the Flowers

INGREDIENTS

Ice
$1/2$ ounce rose vodka
$1/2$ ounce elderflower liqueur
$1/2$ ounce violet liqueur
$1/2$ ounce lemon juice
4 ounces Perrier Jouet Champagne
Spray of rose water
Rose petal garnish

1. Fill a wine glass half with ice.

2. Add the first four ingredients.

3. Add Champagne, then spray the top of the drink with rose water.

4. Add garnish.

Tropical Rainbow Punch

INGREDIENTS

1 750-milliliter chilled bottle coconut rum
$1/2$ gallon chilled pineapple juice
1 pint multicolored sherbet
2 liters chilled ginger ale
Pineapple flags garnish

YIELDS 20–25 SERVINGS

1. Pour the first two ingredients into a pitcher and chill in the fridge.

2. When ready pour chilled mixture into a punch bowl.

3. Set the sherbet in the middle of the punch, then pour in the chilled ginger ale. Add garnish.

Strong Kong

INGREDIENTS

1 ounce Arabica espresso bean and roasted
  cacao nip–infused banana rum
1 ounce coffee liqueur
5 ounces fresh hot coffee
1 teaspoon brown sugar
Pure vanilla extract, whipped cream, and
  Mexican chocolate chunk garnish

1. Pour all the ingredients into a coffee glass.

2. Stir. Add garnish.

If you don't have the time to wait for the cacao nips to infuse your banana rum, just use $1/2$ ounce chocolate liqueur in the recipe. The pure vanilla whipped cream is achieved by adding a cap of pure vanilla as you are whipping the cream. Look for Mexican chocolate in local Spanish or Caribbean stores. This chocolate is unlike any chocolate you've ever tasted. It's mixed with spices and coarse-grained sugar.

Rhuby Slipper

INGREDIENTS

Ice

1$\frac{1}{2}$ ounce rhubarb and strawberry-infused gold rum

1 ounce fresh Persian lime juice

1 ounce falernum

4 ounces dry white wine

2 ounces fresh charged filtered water

Fanned strawberry garnish

1. Fill a medium wine glass half with ice.

2. Add all the ingredients except for the fresh charged water. Stir.

3. Top with fresh charged water. Add garnish.

When infusing the gold rum with rhubarb and strawberries to make the Rhuby Slipper, make sure you do not put the rhubarb leaves into the infusion because they are toxic. The stalk is the only part that is nontoxic. Gardeners know to grow rhubarb on the outskirts of their garden for this reason. Falernum is the sweetening agent in this cocktail. It can be found in gourmet shops or online.

Heatwave

INGREDIENTS

Fresh-ground cinnamon and organic sugar to
 rim glass
Ice
2 ounces rainbow peppercorn-infused mango
 rum
1 ounce tropical fruit puree
1 ounce fresh Meyer lemon juice
2 dashes Angostura bitters
Mini-mango checkerboard cut arched garnish

1. Rim a chilled cocktail glass with the
 cinnamon sugar.

2. Shake all the ingredients with ice.

3. Strain into the glass. Add mini-mango
 garnish.

When infusing the mango rum for the Heat-
wave, crack the peppercorns a little by plac-
ing them in a plastic bag and giving them a
couple of good hits with something heavy. A
variety of peppercorn types can be found in
gourmet stores. Rainbow peppercorn can be
found as a mixture of white, black, pink, and
green peppercorns.

Making frozen dessert drinks is where you can really have some fun.

Coladas and margaritas both benefit from lots of ice and juices, fruits, purees, nectars, liqueurs, and even flavored rums and tequilas. Animal-inspired tropical drinks have always been very popular for parties. It's safe to assume that any drink with the word "monkey" in the name will involve banana.

Do you like devil's food, red velvet, carrot, black forest, pineapple upside-down, or wedding cake? Practically any dessert can be turned into a frozen drink. Simply break down the key elements of the recipe. For example, Banana Cream Pie calls for bananas, milk, sugar, butter, vanilla, and a whipped cream topping. So you can use vanilla vodka, banana liqueur, butterscotch schnapps, half-and-half, and some fresh banana to give it body. Blend it up and top it with whipped cream. Voilá! ●

Piña Colada

Ice
2 ounces Puerto Rican rum
1 ounce coconut cream
3 ounces pineapple juice
Pineapple flag garnish

1. Blend ingredients with a half cup of ice. Add additional ice if needed.

2. Pour into a tropical glass.

3. Add garnish.

If you plan on making a few Piña Coladas for friends and family, then make it easy by premixing a Piña Colada mix. All you need is a pitcher, pineapple juice, and Coco López coconut cream. Fill the pitcher three-quarters full with pineapple juice and then the rest of the way with coconut cream and stir.

Dark rums that contain molasses make the Piña Colada taste like heaven. Many people like to float the dark rum on top or just add it to the blending process.

Miami Vice

INGREDIENTS

Ice
2 ounces light rum
1 ounce coconut cream
3 ounces pineapple juice
4 ounces strawberry daiquiri mix*
Pineapple and strawberry garnish

1. Blend the first three ingredients with a half cup of ice.

2. Pour into a tropical glass.

3. Blend the strawberry daiquiri mix with a half cup of ice.

4. Pour into the glass. Add garnish.

Shake the can of coconut cream before opening because the solids and liquids inside separate.

*See page 120 for a strawberry daiquiri mix recipe.

Melon Colada

INGREDIENTS

Ice
1 ounce light rum
1 ounce melon liqueur
1 ounce coconut cream
3 ounces pineapple juice
Pineapple and cherry garnish

1. Blend ingredients with a half cup of ice. Add additional ice if needed.

2. Pour into a tropical glass.

3. Add garnish.

Flavored PC

You can add fun flavor by adding a liqueur. Other liqueurs that taste great in a Piña Colada are coffee, raspberry, chocolate, banana, peach, and Amaretto. For a fun color, float blue Curaçao on top, and for a lava look, simply pour a colored mix like strawberry into the bottom of the glass before you pour in the Piña Colada.

Independence Colada

INGREDIENTS

$\frac{1}{2}$ ounce grenadine
Ice
1$\frac{1}{2}$ ounces light rum
4 ounces piña colada mix
$\frac{1}{2}$ ounce blue Curaçao

1. Pour the grenadine into the bottom of a tropical glass.

2. Blend the rum and piña colada mix with a cup of ice.

3. Pour into the glass.

4. Float the blue Curaçao on top.

Frozen Daiquiri

INGREDIENTS

Ice
2 ounces light Cuban rum
2 ounces fresh squeezed lime juice
2 ounces simple syrup
Lime garnish

1. Blend ingredients with a half cup of ice. Add additional ice if needed.

2. Pour into stemmed glass.

3. Add garnish.

Flavored daiquiris are very popular party drinks. The most popular is a Strawberry Daiquiri. The next-most popular are peach, raspberry, mango, and banana. Also there are a lot of flavored rums to incorporate into a Classic Daiquiri, such as coconut, orange, raspberry, lemon, spiced, cherry, pineapple, banana, and mango.

Strawberry Daiquiri

INGREDIENTS

Sugar to rim glass (optional)
Ice
2 ounces light rum
4 ounces strawberry daiquiri mix*
Choice of lime, strawberry, or whipped cream
  garnish

YIELDS A HALF GALLON

1. Blend ingredients with a half cup of ice. Add
   additional ice if needed.

2. Pour into stemmed glass.

3. Add preferred garnish. If sugar rim is your
   choice, then make that step 1.

*See page 120 for a strawberry daiquiri mix recipe.

Strawberry Margarita

INGREDIENTS

Ice

2 ounces 100 percent blanco tequila of choice

1 ounce triple sec

1 ounce fresh lime juice

1 ounce simple syrup

2 ounces strawberry mix or puree

Lime and strawberry garnish

1. Blend ingredients with a half cup of ice. Add additional ice if needed.

2. Pour into a margarita glass. Add garnish.

3. You can replace the triple sec with Cointreau.

Strawberry Mix

Strawberry liqueurs are rarely used in a strawberry margarita. Most bars don't stock them, and most liquor stores don't carry them. Learn to make homemade strawberry puree on page 119. Homemade strawberry mix can be found on page 120. Or use lots of fresh, ripe strawberries and a little more simple syrup.

Melon Margarita

Ice
2 ounces 100 percent blanco tequila of choice
1 ounce melon liqueur
$\frac{1}{10}$ ounce fresh lime juice
1 ounce simple syrup
Lime garnish

1. Blend ingredients with a half cup of ice. Add additional ice if needed.

2. Pour into a margarita glass. Add garnish.

3. You can replace the blanco tequila with reposado tequila.

> For every liqueur on the market, there are low-end and high-end choices. Sometimes you can get by with the lower end if you are on a budget. However, when it comes to melon liqueur, it's best to go with Midori. Generic brands can't compare. It's been around since 1978 and came from Japan. The word *midori* is Japanese for "green."

Peach Margarita

INGREDIENTS

Ice
2 ounces 100 percent blanco tequila
1 ounce triple sec
1/10 ounce fresh lime juice
1 ounce simple syrup
2 ounces peach purée
1/2 ounce grenadine
Peach and lime garnish

1. Blend ingredients (except the grenadine) with a half cup of ice.

2. Pour grenadine into the bottom of the glass.

3. Pour the blended mixture into the glass. Add garnish.

4. You can replace the triple sec with Cointreau.

> Normally you don't salt the rim on a fruity margarita; however, some people like the salt on a sweeter margarita. Others will rim the glass in sugar, and still others will make a 1:1 mixture of salt and sugar to rim with. The bottom line is preference.

Blue Coconut Margarita

INGREDIENTS

Shredded coconut rim for glass
Ice
2 ounces coconut Tequila
1 ounce blue Curaçao
$1/_{10}$ ounce fresh lime juice
1 ounce simple syrup

1. Rim a margarita glass with shredded coconut.

2. Blend ingredients with a half cup of ice. Add additional ice if needed.

3. Pour into a margarita glass.

Rimming with coconut flakes requires a little more sticking power than does just rubbing a lemon or lime around the rim and then dipping. And even though simple syrup is very sticky, it's just not quite sticky enough. You'll have to use Karo light syrup. Pour an ounce of Karo syrup onto a saucer, squeeze one lime wedge, and mix together.

Pomegranate Mango Margarita

INGREDIENTS

Ice
2 ounces reposado tequila
1 ounce triple sec
1 ounce fresh lime juice
1 ounce simple syrup
1 ounce mango puree
$1/2$ ounce pomegranate juice

1. Blend ingredients with a cup of ice. Add additional ice if needed.

2. Pour into a margarita glass.

3. You can replace the triple sec with Cointreau.

Hawaiian Margarita

INGREDIENTS

Ice
2 ounces 100 percent agave blanco tequila
1 ounce triple sec
1 ounce fresh lime juice
1 ounce pineapple juice
1 ounce papaya puree
$\frac{1}{2}$ ounce simple syrup
Pineapple garnish

1. **Up:** Shake ingredients with ice. Strain into a chilled cocktail glass.

2. **Rocks:** Shake ingredients with ice. Strain into a margarita glass filled with ice.

3. **Frozen:** Blend ingredients with a half cup of ice. Pour into a margarita glass.

What makes a Hawaiian Margarita Hawaiian is the pineapple and papaya because both are grown in Hawaii. You can replace the papaya with other Hawaiian fruits such as banana, coconut, or mango. This margarita can be served at a tiki-, tropical-, or luau-themed party. Feel free to garnish the drink with plenty of edible flowers and paper parasols.

Chocolate Monkey

INGREDIENTS

Chocolate syrup
1 ounce vanilla vodka
1 ounce banana liqueur
1 ounce white crème de cacao
4 ounces half-and-half
Ice
Whipped cream garnish

1. Squirt some chocolate syrup into a tall glass.

2. Blend ingredients with a half cup of ice. Add additional ice if needed.

3. Pour into the glass. Add garnish.

Frog in a Blender

INGREDIENTS

Chocolate syrup
$1/2$ ounce grenadine
1 ounce white crème de cacao
1 ounce green crème de menthe
4 ounces half-and-half
Ice
Whipped cream garnish

1. Squirt some chocolate syrup into a tall glass.

2. Pour grenadine into the glass.

3. Blend remaining ingredients with a half cup of ice.

4. Pour into the glass. Add garnish.

The Frog in a Blender is a novelty frozen drink. It tastes like a fresh peppermint patty, but it can easily jump all the way to the other end of the spectrum if you insert a rubber frog halfway into the drink and then serve. It's perfect to serve at Halloween! To bump up the alcohol level, add vodka or chocolate vodka.

Fresh Funky Monkey

INGREDIENTS

2 ounces organic chocolate syrup
Filtered ice
2 ounces organic rum
1 organic banana
3 ounces organic soy milk
Organic shaved chocolate garnish

1. Squirt 1 ounce of the organic chocolate syrup into half a tall glass.

2. Pour the rest of the ingredients into a blender with a cup of ice and blend.

3. Pour into the glass. Add garnish.

> Don't forget that you can infuse organic spirits with organic products. For example, for the Fresh Funky Monkey, you could make infused banana rum. Or make chocolate rum. Vanilla rum would be yummy, too, by using organic vanilla pods. Also available is organic chocolate soy milk.

Down the Rabbit Hole

INGREDIENTS

Filtered ice
2 ounces organic vodka
2 ounces organic carrot juice
1 ounce pomegranate juice
1 ounce organic raw honey
4 ounces organic yogurt
2 ounces kefir
Handful of organic blueberries
Organic carrot stick and blueberries garnish

1. Blend ingredients with a cup of filtered ice. Add additional ice if needed.

2. Taste to determine sweetness. If preferred sweeter, simply add more honey.

3. Pour into a stemmed glass. Add garnish.

Banana Cream Pie

INGREDIENTS

Karo syrup to paint glass
Crushed graham cracker
1 ounce vanilla vodka
1 ounce banana liqueur
$\frac{1}{2}$ ounce butterscotch schnapps
Half a banana
4 ounces half-and-half
Ice
Whipped cream garnish

1. Paint half the inside of a tall glass with Karo syrup.

2. Sprinkle with graham cracker crumbs.

3. Blend ingredients with a half cup of ice.

4. Pour into the glass. Add whipped cream garnish.

FROM THE BLENDER

Strawberry Shortcake

INGREDIENTS

Whipped cream
1 ounce vodka
1 ounce Amaretto
2 ounces half-and-half
2 ounces strawberry mix
Ice
Strawberry garnish

1. Squirt whipped cream into the bottom of a tall glass.

2. Blend ingredients with a half cup of ice.

3. Pour into the glass. Add whipped cream garnish.

Did you know that between 1840 and 1880 people all over America threw strawberry shortcake parties at the beginning of summer? Until that time, strawberries—like many things—were available only seasonally and locally. Then modern technology—the railroad—roared through the country. For the first time, strawberries could be shipped in icebox cars from coast to coast.

German Chocolate Cake

INGREDIENTS

Shredded coconut and chocolate syrup
1 ounce coconut rum
1 ounce dark crème de cacao
$1/2$ ounce hazelnut liqueur
1 scoop chocolate ice cream
1 ounce half-and-half
Ice
Whipped cream, and chocolate shavings garnish

1. Rim a tall glass with chocolate syrup and shredded coconut.

2. Blend ingredients with a half cup of ice.

3. Pour into the glass. Add garnish.

Place Your Bet

If you bet that German Chocolate Cake originated in Germany and was created by a stout German woman in her kitchen, well, you'd lose. A Texas homemaker who sent the recipe to her local newspaper in 1957 created it. The recipe used Baker's German Sweet Chocolate, a brand created by an Englishman in 1852.

Infusing flavors into rum couldn't be easier.

Infused Rum

INGREDIENTS

1 750-milliliter bottle premium light rum
3 vanilla beans cut and scraped

1. Pour the rum into a sterile, wide-mouthed jar.

2. Add vanilla pods. Seal jar.

3. Set in a dark cool place and agitate once daily for four days.

4. Strain and funnel into a sterile jar or bottle.

Stronger flavors that take only three to four days include vanilla, citrus rinds, and lavender. Edibles that take up to a week include pitted cherries, figs, dates, apples, raspberries, rose petals, watermelon, peaches, lychees, strawberries, blueberries, blackberries, mangos, and papaya. Fibrous edibles like ginger, pineapple, cinnamon sticks, and whole cloves take up to two weeks. If you combine flavors, then you may not be able to put them in at the same time.

Purees add bursting, concentrated flavor to a cocktail.

To make a puree, just peel and chop your chosen carbohydrate, steam it, and mash it in a food processor. You can now mix in more ingredients or other purees if desired. Spoon puree into small sterile jars and refrigerate.

Tropical Puree

INGREDIENTS

1 mango peeled, pitted, and chopped
1 cup chopped fresh pineapple
1 ripe banana
1 ounce simple syrup or falernum if desired

YIELDS 1 CUP

1. Steam mango and pineapple until soft.

2. Place in the food processor with the banana for 1 minute.

3. Taste, then add simple syrup or falernum if desired.

4. Spoon into sterile jars or containers. Refrigerate.

Strawberry Daiquiri Mix

INGREDIENTS

2 cups sugar
2 cups lukewarm water
I cup freshly squeezed lime juice
4 cups ripe (or frozen) strawberries

YIELDS A HALF GALLON

1. Combine the sugar and water in a large
    jar and shake the jar until all the sugar has
    dissolved.

2. Cut the tops off the ripe strawberries
    and wash well, or you can use frozen
    strawberries.

3. Fill blender with half the strawberries, then
    pour in half of the lime juice and half of the
    sugar water and blend. Keep adding and
    blending ingredients to make a pourable mix.
    Taste as you go. You may not need all the
    sugar water, depending on the ripeness of
    the strawberries. Pour into a container and
    keep in the fridge.